First published in Great Britain in 1984 by
Octopus Books Limited under the title *Animal 1 2 3*

This edition published in 1989 by
Treasure Press
Michelin House
81 Fulham Road
London SW3 6RB

© 1984 Octopus Books Limited

ISBN 1 85051 358 9

Printed in Portugal

MY FIRST 123 BOOK

Illustrated by

Elphin Lloyd-Jones

TREASURE PRESS

1
over-eating orang-utan

Orang-utans live in the trees on
two tropical islands, Sumatra
and Borneo. They use their
strong arms to swing from one
tree branch to another.

2
talking toucans

Toucans live in the jungles of South and Central America. Toucans are famous for their large, bright-coloured beaks. They use them to pick and open the fruit they eat.

3
timid tigers

Tigers are the largest of the big cats. They live in the jungles of Asia, where they silently hunt animals.

4
flirting flamingos

Flamingos stand on their long legs and dip their curved beaks into the water to catch fish. They live in colonies, which sometimes have as many as 900,000 pairs of birds.

5
frying frogs

Frogs spend part of their lives
in water and part on dry land.
In the water, they breathe with
gills as fish do. On land, they
breathe with lungs as mammals do.

6
swaying snakes

Snakes have no legs, no eyelids,
and no ears. They move by
slithering along the ground.
Some snakes are poisonous, but
most are harmless.

7
see sawing seals

Seals hunt for food in the water
using their powerful flippers
to swim. They come ashore to
rest and sleep.

8
elegant elephants

Elephants are the largest of all
land animals. They use their
long trunks to lift food up
to their mouths.

9
noisy newts

Like frogs, newts live in the water and on land. They spend most of the time on land, where they catch insects and worms for food.

10
tackling tabbies

Cats purr when they are happy
and hiss when they are angry.
A "tabby" is a grey or brown cat
with dark stripes.

11
entertaining emus

Emus live in Australia. They
have wings but cannot fly. To
escape danger, they run quickly
on their strong legs.

12
tunnelling tapirs

Tapirs have short legs and long noses, like small elephants' trunks. They live in the jungle and are active at night.

13
thirsty thrushes

Thrushes are found all over the world, except at the North and South Poles. They are among the best singers of all birds, and they can imitate the songs of many other birds.

14
fencing foxes

Foxes belong to the same animal
family as dogs. They usually
hunt at night, but sometimes
in spring they come out during
the day.

15
flying fishes

Flying fish have fins which
open out like birds' wings.
When they are in danger, they
leap out of the water and glide
through the air on their fins.

16
snoring snails

Most snails have large shells
that protect them from other
animals. Some live on land and
others live at the bottom of
the sea or in lakes and rivers.

17
stretching sloths

Sloths live in the trees of South
and Central America. They
hang upside down, holding on
with their powerful arms.
Because they live upside down,
their fur grows the opposite way
from other animals.

18
eager eagles

Eagles are sometimes called "The King of Birds." They fly high in the sky and swoop down at great speed to grab the animals they hunt.

19
naughty nags

"Nags" is another name for horses. In days gone by, horses used to pull coaches and carriages. Today, horseback riding is one of the most popular of all sports.